In the Wake of The Hurricane
National Edition

by Bob Ogley

The wind that blew in from the sea in the early hours of October 16, 1987 and changed the face of southern England prompted newspaper editor, Bob Ogley to produce an instant book showing the devastation in a large area of West Kent and beyond. In little more than a month In The Wake Of The Hurricane sold 25,000 copies and was a best-seller in a dozen towns. This new book, produced by popular demand, will have a wider appeal. It traces the story of one of the greatest storms ever to hit our shores and describes how those of us in this heavily populated, but normally insulated, area of Western Europe now have a far greater respect for the forces of nature.

GUILD PUBLISHING LONDON

Part of the proceeds from the sale of this book will be donated to The National Trust Trees and Gardens Storm Disaster Appeal.

To Fern with much Love

This edition published 1989 by
Guild Publishing
by arrangement with
Froglets Publications Limited
Brasted Chart
Westerham, Kent, TN16 1LY

First Impression March 1988
Reprinted March, April, May, 1988
Revised edition September 1988
Reprinted in hardback October 1988

© Bob Ogley 1988

CN 9789

Jacket illustrations
Front cover photograph: Knole Park, Sevenoaks — Storm tossed by Les Hunt
Back cover photograph: Seal Chart by Roger Tutt

Cover illustrations
Front cover photograph: The view North from Emmetts House,
by Eric Crichton, National Trust
Back cover photograph: Seal Chart by Roger Tutt.

Typeset by Typecast Ltd, East Peckham, Kent, TN12 5HF
Printed and bound in Great Britain by
Staples Printers (Rochester) Ltd, Love Lane, Rochester, Kent, ME1 1TP

The preparation of this book would not have been possible without the help of a variety of sources. All of them were competent, helpful and patient in marked degree and I owe them my thanks.

Courier Newspaper Group
The Meteorological Office
Dundee University
Jersey Evening Post
Brighton Evening Argus
The News, Portsmouth
The Surrey Mirror
Evening Echo, Basildon
East Anglian Daily Times
Daily Express
Press Association
Kent Messenger
Kentish Times
Isle of Thanet Gazette
Surrey Advertiser
Eastern Daily Press
The National Trust
Sevenoaks District Council
Daily Telegraph
The Observer
The Sunday Times
South Eastern Electricity Board
The Daily Mail
British Rail Network South-East

I would also like to thank the following individuals for their excellent contributions: Hazel Pelling, Fiona MacLeod, Fiona Baird-Murray, Roger Tutt, Michael Knights, Arland Kingston, Phillip Lane, Les Hunt, David Court, David Bennett, Gordon Anckorn, Alex Watson, Neil Nevison, Peter Tilley, Michael Wheeler, Paul Amos, Lynn McCracken, Douglas Nye, Jon Rodwell, Sean Brown, Nicholas Sapieha, Patsy Fagan, David Sache, Eric Crichton and Mike Howarth.

Introduction

OCTOBER 16, 1987 is a date we shall all remember. It will be talked about by future generations as the time when nature's naked fury hurled itself at southern England and in many areas completely changed the face of the landscape.

As dawn came to the town and countryside on that fateful morning it was difficult to believe that many familiar scenes on which dusk had fallen the night before had vanished for ever.

In those few short hours 15 million trees were blown down and giants which had stood for 200, 300 or even 400 years lay prostrate on the ground, their vast rain-sodden roots towering in the air. Telephone posts were upended, water and gas supplies cut; ships were tossed on to the shore and a hundred thousand miles of road were blocked by fallen trees. There was no electricity in millions of homes. It was the worst power failure since the second world war.

Coming in from the Channel Islands, the storm touched land at the border of Devon and Dorset, then moved steadily north-east in a gigantic swathe across the country to The Wash. In those terrifying hours skylines were changed and the great wooded areas of south and east England were left looking as if they had been raped and indecently exposed.

This book traces the devastation and shows the terrible damage inflicted in an area covering thousands of square miles. However it is more than a record of destruction and chaos. It is also a story of resourcefulness and bravery and shows how we picked ourselves up and carried on in the most impossible circumstances.

Life now may seem to be normal, but there is nothing normal about our parks, woodlands and gardens which have been nurtured with such loving care through the centuries. They look like battlefields in the aftermath of an artillery bombardment and it is going to take many more months to clear the way so that replanting may begin.

From little acorns, giant oaks will grow. As we watch them mature we shall never forget Friday October 16, 1987 — our date with history.

Contents

Battered by 90 mph winds, Sealink's cross-channel ferry ship, Hengist broke away from her moorings in Folkestone Harbour early on Friday morning, October 16. Captain Sid Bridgewater gave orders to sail out of the harbour but the sea was rolling so violently that the engines, completely waterlogged, cut out and the ship was plunged into darkness. She rolled around helplessly with the Captain and 24 crew members fearing the worst. At 5 am, the Hengist was blown onto the rocks just below The Warren at Folkestone where she stayed, firmly aground, until the following Thursday. The damage to the keel and cabins has now been repaired and the Hengist is back on her cross-channel run.

Re-Planting Our Heritage

by Winston S. Churchill MP

Sir Winston Churchill looks out over the Chartwell lakes to the woods beyond. His grandson writes. "It was a mercy my grandfather was no longer around to witness the scenes of devastation."

MUCH of the glory of Kent has always been its stock of old and magnificent trees. While other parts of the country have been denuded of trees over recent generations or seen their hardwood trees replaced by grim plantations of little conifers, the Kent countryside has, to a remarkable extent, retained its character and its Englishness with its wonderful hardwood trees, especially its oaks and beeches.

The devastation caused by the Great Storm which struck Kent in the early hours of 16 October, wreaked terrible devastation on Chartwell and the neighbouring areas of Crockham Hill, Toys Hill and Ide Hill, standing on the ridge line where they were especially exposed.

One of the great glories of Chartwell was the spectacular horse-shoe of tall beech trees standing proudly on the hills surrounding the valley and framing its view dominating the Weald of Kent. In the autumn sunlight the trees would make a brilliant shimmering backdrop of yellow, orange, red and gold, to one of the finest views in England. This year there are no leaves to reflect and enhance the brilliance of the scene; there are no trees. The great beeches lie snapped and stricken on all sides like so much match-wood. It was a mercy that my Grandfather was no longer around to witness the scenes of devastation in the valley that he loved so much and which he and my Grandmother made their family home for more than 40 years of their lives — he would have been inconsolable.

It will take years to remove the stricken giants and clear the débris. It will take many generations for Chartwell and the surrounding area to be restored to its former glory. But we who know and have loved the glorious heritage which has been ours in this special part of Kent, owe it to future generations to replant for the future on a scale never done before and to replant not with little Scandinavian conifers but with the magnificent trees of Old England, the beech, the ash and the English oak so that future generations may enjoy their splendours as we have done.

Residents in the beautiful tree-lined avenue at Route Orange in Jersey had to be evacuated in the height of the storm. Between 60 and 80 people spent the night at Les Quennevais School. These amazing pictures, before and after, tell the tragic story.

The Night of the Hurricane

THERE was nothing particularly unusual about the evening of Thursday October 15, 1987. Rain which had been lashing down in torrents all day long had stopped but throughout southern England the skies were still heavy with rain and dusk came quickly. It was a moonless, cheerless windy October night.

In many river valleys where the waters were dangerously high a Grade B flood alert needed careful monitoring. Police inspectors wanted their men to be extra vigilant and firemen prepared for a busy night. People living by the waterfront sandbagged their homes. In outlying communities farmers were concerned for their sheep as the waters lapped into fields. Coastguards anticipated a wild night but were thankful that the high tides had passed.

High in the hills, on the ridges, downs, charts and even the forests, families felt secure. No flood waters could rise to several hundred feet. In such bad weather trees were like friendly soldiers and those which guarded the hillside homes on this October night rustled in the breeze. It had been windy all day.

The weathermen had warned of severe gusts. They were keeping their eyes on the Bay of Biscay where the depression was centring. France was enduring heavy winds which seemed to be heading towards the Channel, northern France and the low countries. Harbourmasters urged boat owners to check their craft. Whatever else, it was not a night to be at sea.

During the evening the wind blew with some force but there was no undue alarm and the people slept with the assurance that life would be the same in the morning.

At the mouth of the Bristol Channel the depression deepened dramatically. Between midnight and 6 am, towns, cities, villages, islands and the countryside endured the most furious gale ever known, the wind reaching speeds of more than 100 miles an hour. This was a hurricane; the omnipotent hand of God tearing at both townscape and landscape and changing it for ever.

Couples in bed huddled together for comfort as the wind came in gusts of deafening ferocity. Many families moved to safe rooms or cellars taking their children with them. People living alone were petrified. Others just waited fearing their homes would be carried away by the wind.

The hurricane attacked in waves starting with a faraway growl and building up to a frightening roar as it blasted everything in its path. The roar drowned the crunch of falling trees. It drowned the sound of tiles and slates being ripped away. Limbs from trees flew in the air and petrified animals instinctively sought shelter in young coppices, away from the swaying giants.

Chimney pots crashed, walls fell apart and this furious night was illuminated with constant flashes as trees toppled onto power cables.

At the height of the storm the National Grid failed blacking out all southern England including London. Phones went dead but the roar continued. In the Channel Islands and along the south coast hotels and buildings collapsed trapping people inside. Parish church spires tumbled down in a tangle of twisted timbers. Gravestones were lifted in cemeteries, headstones smashed and crosses cracked. Dinghies and boats in reservoirs and lakes were thrown together in a giant's junk yard scene. Cranes toppled on to the road. The M4 was brought to a standstill with the elevated section in West London closed. The M25 was blocked in many places. Many towns and villages were completely cut off. Airports closed and trains came to a standstill.

Two firemen were killed in Dorset, men and women died as chimney stacks caved in and drivers perished as trees fell across cars. In the woodlands and on those "safe" hills, God played his giant game of skittles.

Dawn came uneasily with the wind blowing but the hurricane gone. Many people went back to bed as if putting off that dreadful moment that was to change their lives. As a more civilised hour approached and the gusts finally subsided, front doors opened.

The scenes were unbelievable.

Stories of the Night

EVERYBODY in the path of the storm will remember vividly the early hours of October 16, 1987. It was the night many people thought the world was coming to an end as the hurricane winds approaching in terrifying bursts threatened to lift the roofs of houses right across southern England.

Nineteen people lost their lives, a tragic but nonetheless miraculously low toll considering the magnitude of the diaster and the unprecedented material losses. Vast industrial complexes were badly damaged including gas works and power stations. Railways were out of action and thousands of miles of roads were blocked by fallen trees.

The whole world heard the story of England's great storm and in many cases TV viewers received the wrong information. Italians were told that the death toll ran into thousands and holidaymakers in Spain were horrified to hear that the town of Sevenoaks had been flattened and homes blown off the face of the earth.

Frantic long distance telephone calls to the town, blocked for several days by fallen wires, finally revealed the truth which had been lost in translation. Six of the seven oak trees had gone. The town at least remained.

Scores of people in the storm battered south will never know how they survived the night. Many policemen and firemen were on duty. Farmers were in the fields tending their livestock. Long distance lorry drivers were playing dodgems with scurrying branches and sap was smearing itself on the windscreen. A few motorists were on the road, anxious to get home but terrified of the wind which was blowing them broadside. One boy at least clambered over horizontal trees carrying his bicycle and near Redhill 200 passengers were trapped in a train.

The experiences of these people exposes in great detail the full horror of the night but it also shows the exceptional endeavour and resourcefulness of those caught by the storm.

The 1 am Victoria to Gatwick train, carrying many holidaymakers, ran into a fallen tree as it approached Merstham tunnel in Surrey and frightened passengers waited two hours in the darkness before an electric train arrived to shunt them out. This in turn was damaged by falling trees so the passengers got off without luggage and walked along the track with everything crashing around them. In order to get onto the platform at Merstham station they had to axe down a gate and then waited until 4 am for a diesel train to take them to Redhill. The passengers, many now in a state of near collapse, were escorted to Redhill Post Office canteen where they were given a cup of tea in conditions resembling an air raid. The drama continued. The canteen was plunged into darkness as power failed and the passengers had to return to the train for security reasons. There they lay on the floor until the storm subsided.

At Bexley in Kent teenager Kelly Ford of Sibley Close was buried under a pile of rubble as a tree crashed on his bedroom. He refused to panic as his father dug him out with considerable care.

This was a story repeated all over southern England. At Ramsgate a woman was trapped when a chimney stack crashed through the ceiling of her home in Chapel Place. June Mulgrew's husband worked frantically to free her while her son Toby ran into the darkness for help. At the same time Wpc Alison Sheer and Pc Gary Lux of Ramsgate were driving through the night with trees crashing around them in order to rescue an injured baby in Ash, 10 miles away.

At Sevenoaks, Chief Inspector Mick Lofthouse and Pc Stephen Griffiths drove to the village of Otford to check for floods just as the hurricane blew in. "It was like world war three said Mr Lofthouse. Trees were crashing all around us and I didn't think we would make it back to the station". Power cables started arcing and the flashes of a few thousand volts made it look like a science fiction film or an invasion from Mars. The two policemen were terrified. The only way they could get back to the station was via the Otford flyover but a tree crashed down in front and behind them trapping them in the middle. The officers scrambled through branches and made their way on foot to the police station where the chief inspector called all his men off the road.

If the officers were frightened so too was Mrs Julie Pell of Saxby's, Cowden whose baby decided at the height of the storm it was time to make an appearance in this terrifying world. Julie and husband John set off in their car for Pembury Hospital in Kent but also became trapped between two fallen trees. At three in the morning they abandoned their car and walked home, clambering over trees and wind-blown débris. By the time they reached their house Julie was in the second stage of labour but fortunately an intrepid doctor from Edenbridge reached Cowden by climbing the fallen trees. Baby Andrea arrived at 11 am.

Marilyn Price from Blackham, Sussex also had an imminent arrival and also found the route to the hospital blocked. Her plight was such that a helicopter was called. It touched down outside her cottage and flew to a playing field near the hospital where an ambulance rushed Marilyn to the maternity ward. Baby Simon was born at 7.45 pm on Friday October 16.

The Observer motoring correspondent Douglas Nye with some urgent copy for his newspaper decided to drive from Farnham in Surrey to London at 2 am on the Friday morning. He first appreciated the storm's severity when a sustained cannonade of twigs and branches heaved his car broadside and a disembowelled traffic bollard trailing broken wires bounded across his path.

Having exchanged grimaces with a taxi driver, delivered his copy, dodged rumbling dustbins and flying glass, Mr Nye drove back home into the teeth of the storm. He described the scene at Twickenham. "The dual carriageway there had become just a quivering, twitching, shaggy green carpet of twigs and leaves. Larger boughs, fallen trees humped into view, projecting tentacles flailing in the gale. I had to weave lock-to-lock dodging the major obstacles".

A car in front took a bough on its left front. The driver stopped. Mr Nye said: "It was like a torpedoed ship reeling away from a wartime convoy, leaving its consorts to struggle on".

At one stage near Sunbury his front wheels were lifted from the road. He rounded trees by driving on kerbs and verges and eventually arrived home unscathed but considered his survival to be a lottery.

In North Kent near Wrotham, Wendy Bardell and her husband Trevor lay awake listening to the build-up of the wind. In another bedroom was daughter Clowey, aged six. Outside, within a few feet of the house, a 125 foot beech tree was rocking violently. Wendy despatched Trevor with torch into the garden to check the scene.

He returned and they lay awake in bed listening to the radio waiting for the storm to die out. Suddenly there was the most terrifying ears-plintering crash. Wendy saw the light of dawn open above her. Briefly there was sky and then darkness again as roof tiles, masonry, jagged branches, plaster and rubble rained down on top of her.

Wendy writes: "Even today I can hear my own screams and remember how I instinctively found the strength to remove great weights and scramble free. I was covered in blood but Trevor escaped unscathed. The bedroom, full of debris and broken glass had provided the resting place for our magnificent beech. At that moment our lives, too, were uprooted".

Paul Meredith of Brasted Chart, near Westerham will re-live the hours of Friday October 16 over and over again. Having inspected the trees around the house he took his wife Maggie and children, Hannah, Rebecca and Marcus to the bottom of the garden where, wrapped in duvets, they spent the rest of the night with a hurricane for company.

A beech tree which had worried Mr Meredith had crashed on the house splintering the upper storey. One of the main limbs had pierced the mattress on Rebecca's bed and anxious neighbours looking at the house feared the worse until the family emerged from the garden.

The Rev Harry Forder of Grove Cottage, Levylsdene, near Guildford also left his bedroom — but the circumstances were more terrifying. A tree crashed on his house and he fell through the floor, landing in the hall next to the telephone. Somehow he managed to pick himself up and dial 999; Then the phone went dead.

Mrs Forder said: "It was frightening. The roof was falling around me and my legs were trapped by beams. I was trying to search around for something to put over my head to protect myself. But nothing fell on my head. I called to my husband and he was all right. Then we heard George, the dog, bark.

The couple who had only lived in the house for two weeks were rescued by firemen. They could not be taken to hospital because the road was blocked by fallen trees. Was the Rev Forder lucky? No, he said, You make your own luck. This was a miracle.

A miracle too for Waterlooville mother Mrs Sandra Knight who lay on one half of the bed and watched in terror as a giant oak tree selected the other half. "It was like a thunderbolt. I just screamed and dived out," she said.

For Barbara and Terry Coleman of Corton Long Lane, Lowestoft it wasn't a solitary tree that disturbed their night — it was nine.

At 6 am they were outside when a beech came down in front of the house blocking the front door. They crawled underneath and sat in the dining room when a bigger beech hit the back of the house, blocking the back door. An oak tree then came down on top of the second beech. Two more oaks hit the garage and as Barbara and Terry cowered in their cottage three more trees fell outside.

Red Cross volunteers throughout Southern England found themselves dealing with unusual requests. They fought their way to isolated homes to comfort the elderly. They opened reception centres in order to provide warmth and company. They came to the rescue of those with holes in their roofs and no idea what to do.

Tarpaulins and blankets from the Red Cross international warehouse, normally used for international disasters were handed out wherever necessary. Gas cylinders were issued to people likely to be without power for several weeks and food, given by people who had no power to run their freezers, was cooked in the Red Cross centres and distributed to the needy.

Members of the WRVS also found themselves in great demand. They toured their areas every day supplying hot soup and food to the men clearing roads. The stoic cheerfulness of all these people will never be forgotten.

Xiang is a seven-year-old Clouded Leopard who escaped during the storm from Howletts Zoo Park, Canterbury. He was eventually reunited with his keeper as this delightful picture shows. See page 125.

The Morning After

BLEARY-EYED from lack of sleep but adrenalin pumping with the excitement of the night, the people of southern England woke to a strange quiet world on Friday October 16 and surveyed the scenes of devastation. At first it seemed like a personal tragedy. A tree on the car, a gaping hole in the roof, an outbuilding in ruins, an apple tree uprooted.

Further inspection revealed the dramatic truth. Familiar scenes on which dusk had fallen a few hours earlier had gone for ever. The hurricane winds had felled giant trees like matchsticks, ripped off roofs, brought down electricity pylons and left telephone wires in tangled, twisted, snake-like coils along country lanes.

Neighbours gathered in the road, some weaving their way through the branches of a tree that had stood proud and upright for perhaps a 100 years or more. "Are you safe?" Is your house damaged?" "Are your children all right?". There were plenty of questions on this unforgettable morning.

In living memory there had never been a storm like it and in rural areas it gradually became apparent that many villages were paralysed. No milk, no papers, no power, no communications, no birds singing.

For those in towns and sheltered areas the realisation came even more slowly. No trains, no cars in the station car parks, no petrol, no rumbling of traffic. This was, indeed, no ordinary morning.

The first sights were of fallen trees everywhere and mile upon mile of them in the villages. The first smells were of crushed pine and beechleaf, a fragrance that was to permeate the air for several days. The first noises were the rasping of chainsaws, mounting in volume as the morning wore on. The first thoughts were of isolation and how to survive it.

In the council offices of major towns chief officers set up their emergency control centres in the nearest conditions to a nuclear disaster they may ever see. In many cases no telephone lines were working and staff had to start the difficult task of collating information and responding to the most pressing problems. Communication was the first priority.

Some local authorities were able to enlist the help of Raynet, the emergency amateur radio group. Others made contact with their county councils and trickles of information revealed the massive extent of road damage. Priorities were established. Homeless units were set up, void council houses made available, contact made with the elderly and the most isolated, and hospitals checked for available beds.

Immediate dangers including the possibility of flooding in low-lying areas due to inoperative pumps, blocked sewers and rivers swollen by several days of incessant rain. Council workmen assisted by voluntary groups and contractors began to cut their way through the jungle.

The control centres enlisted the help of police liaison officers and contacted their MP's for further advice. Home secretary Douglas Hurd declined to declare a state of emergency but some Members of Parliament, cutting through official reticence, were able to persuade the Ministry of Defence that the situations constituted an emergency.

Soldiers from a dozen regiments with a convoy of diggers, bulldozers, army personnel vehicles and jeeps left their barracks to join the chainsaw volunteers and other heroes. The Red Cross, fire brigade, WRVS, social service workers, railway engineers, traders, publicans, vicars, farmers and neighbours all played their part in providing help, warmth and kindness.

Southern England was only temporarily beaten by the hurricane.

This photograph from the Satellite tracking station at Dundee University was taken at 0400 hours and shows the centre of the depression north of London.

Where the Winds Blew

WHERE other countries have climates, we in Britain just have weather, a daily phenomenon that controls our lives, provides a perpetual topic of conversation and is totally unpredictable.

The year, 1987, will go down in history as one of the most unpredictable of all. There were the blizzards of January when many of us were without power or telephone for several days, the warmest April since 1947, the long damp month of June when it rained almost every day, the floods of early October and then finally The Great Storm which was certainly the meteorological event of the century.

Was it a hurricane? No, says the London Weather Centre. A hurricane is the name given to tropical cyclones in the Caribbean and the storm which hit southern England on October 16 was not a cyclone but a vigorous mid-latitude depression which intensified abruptly somewhere near the Bay of Biscay.

Yes, says the Concise Oxford Dictionary. A hurricane is a storm with wind velocity of 75 miles an hour or over. The winds in some areas on October 16 exceeded 100 mph.

At 9.0 pm on Thursday evening October 15, 1987 a depression (low) of central pressure 972 millibars was centred over the north of East Anglia. From this depression a frontal zone lay across the south of England to another depression which was believed to be centred over the western entrance to the English Channel with a central pressure less than 966 millibars.

To the south of the frontal zone the air was quite mild and winds were blowing between south and southwest. The air to the north of the frontal zone was cooler and winds were from the north west.

By 1.0 am on Friday morning the depression in the English Channel had deepened and was centred over the south coast of Cornwall. The associated front was being forced to move quickly northwards over the south of England. With the frontal zone was a broad band of heavy rain.

The depression was over Avon at 3. am and moving rapidly northeastwards reaching Humberside by 6.0. At 9.0 am it was already well out into the North Sea.

The whole of the south of England except the coasts of Sussex and Kent were experiencing light to moderate winds at 9.0 pm on the Thursday evening. They blew in from the south east but the stronger winds which were already affecting the coasts of Sussex and Kent came from the south west.

By 10 pm on Thursday the stronger winds had spread quickly northwards, spreading over the south of England. In inland areas gusts of 46 miles an hour were frequently being reported.

As the depression moved inland and its pressure continued to fall, the winds increased in ferocity over the whole of southern England. At 2.0 am they reached 92 mph on the Sussex coast and by 4.0 am in Hampshire, Sussex and Kent it was approaching 100 mph. London's strongest winds occurred between the hours of 2.0 and 3.0 am.

By 6.0 am a broad belt of exceptionally strong winds covered most of England south of a line from the Severn Estuary to the Wash. Sussex and Kent in particular was being "blown to pieces". By now it was at its strongest in Essex and East Anglia but to the west in the Midlands it was less than 40 mph.

The storm moved into the North Sea and by the Saturday October 17 had reached the Norwegian Sea and weakened.

As hundreds of thousands of people throughout southern England know the wind blew in furious gusts lasting several seconds with calmer periods between.

The trees in October had not yet lost their leaves and so presented a large resistance to the wind. This, and the fact that their roots were less secure because of the waterlogged ground was the reason they suffered so badly.

The Met Office failure to forecast the gales correctly was described by Nicholas Ridley, Secretary of State for the Environment as "unbelievable". At noon on Thursday the track of the depression and its associated frontal systems across Britain was correctly forecast.

The Met Office then predicted that the depression would be over Brittany at 6.0 pm (Thursday), southwest of The Wash at midnight and out in the North Sea by 6.0 am on Friday.

These predictions were based on just one shipboard observation in the Atlantic to the north of Corunna in Spain. It is Britain's only weather ship. In the 1970's there were eight in the North Atlantic.

The Met Office believe that they would have forecast the gales correctly if they still had a weather ship in the Bay of Biscay but The Romeo which used to occupy this station was withdrawn two years ago.

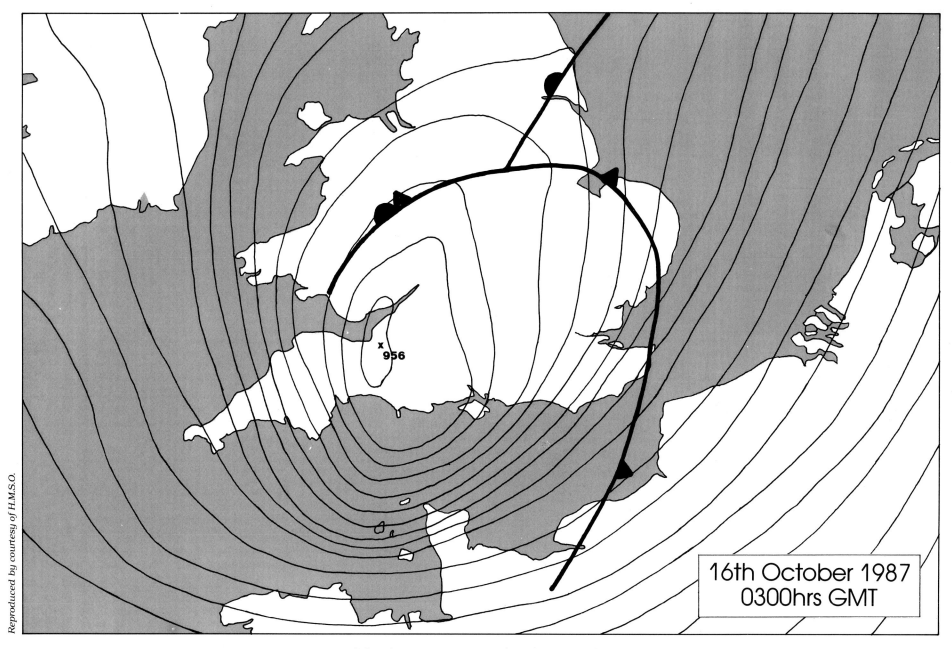

x
956

16th October 1987
0300hrs GMT

On the morning of October 16, 1987 the centre of the depression crossed Britain in a line roughly from Exeter to Scarborough. This map shows the position at 3.00am. The strongest winds were at a distance of about 100 miles south and east of the centre, as is clearly shown here.

Photograph: Courier Newspapers

The oak trees on the northern perimeter of Sevenoaks Vine Cricket ground in Kent were planted in 1902 to commemorate the coronation of Edward VII and so keep alive the tradition of having seven oak trees in the town. They are pictured here in full summer glory.

16

Six of the seven majestic oaks crashed down in the force of the storm and plans were made immediately to have them replaced. A "Hurricane Fayre" was held on Sevenoaks Vine on December 6, 1987 and seven sapling trees planted. Now there are eight oaks, the survivor remaining as a symbol of the night.

Hotels in the Channel Islands suffered extensive damage and many roofs were blown away, in this case the wind carrying it several yards to a field beyond.

This is Clarence Parade, Portsmouth which was one of the first places on England's mainland to meet the full impact of the savage winds. Guests in seafront hotels were devastated by the sight which greeted them in the morning.

The aftermath of the hurricane at Park Avenue, Orpington, Kent. Giant trees which had dominated the pleasant detached houses lie prostrate across the road their uppermost branches reaching gardens on the other side. Notice the milk float in the foreground and how its journey has been rudely interrupted. A car in front has taken the full impact of the tree.

Crunch! This is Surrey on the morning of October 16, Two cars and a garage at Cronks Hill, Reigate are destroyed with a single blow.

The fury of the storm is no better illustrated than in this dramatic photograph at Peacehaven on the Sussex coast. Furniture lies amongst the rubble and the bungalows are devastated.

The scaffolding around this building in Battersea, London buckled and bowed as the wind's ripped through surburban streets.
Few temporary structures such as this survived in the teeth of the gale.

The hangar at Southend airport collapsed wrecking the aircraft inside.

The remains of the Baptist Chapel at Cransford, Suffolk.

The Channel Islands

THE Channel Islands of Jersey, Guernsey, Alderney and Sark were the first to feel the full fury of the storm — and how! Roofs were ripped off apartment blocks and hotels, cars were crushed and tumbling trees changed the landscape beyond recognition.

Many were injured as the roofs and chimneys caved in. Motorists were trapped in their cars and dozens were lucky to escape as walls, fences, masonry and other missiles hurtled through the air before littering the battleground.

The storm hit the Channel Islands just after midnight when almost the first incident was the evacuation of residents in Route Orange, Jersey whose homes were in danger from falling trees.

Two men were trapped in their cars, a woman was blown over a wall and two firemen were hurt as a tree fell on to the house to which they had just been called. In Guernsey and Jersey practically all glasshouses were flattened and the electricity supply to Sark failed shortly before 2 am.

Although several hundred islanders in Jersey were without electricity their power supplies fared better than those in southern England and France. With storms imminent the chief engineer of the Jersey Electricity Council had made the decision to take the French cable link out of service and to restore a generator plant. After that only overhead lines suffered from crashing trees.

As 85 per cent of Jersey's telephone cables are also underground Telecom had few problems but for the islands' insurance agencies the nightmare lasted for many weeks. Hundreds of homes, hotels, shops and factories were so badly battered that essential repairs had to be effected before claims were made.

In the harbours boat owners spent a wild and chaotic night attending their craft, often without any luck. Masts were broken off, sails torn apart and boats broke their moorings to be smashed against the harbour walls. At the La Collette Marina fishermen were unable to reach their boats because the dinghies had sunk. At the Old Pierhead a yacht broke free and sank, dragging three fishing boats with it.

There was one consolation. Had the storm arrived a week earlier during the high tides it is possible the islands would have been flooded; the damage and tragedy colossal.

Photograph: Jersey Evening Post

Adam and Tatiana, aged four and eight, had a miraculous escape when a chimney crashed through the roof of their bedroom in Jersey, burying them in rubble. They were rescued by the fire brigade.

This was the scene that faced commercial growers all over the islands of Guernsey and Jersey.

Maple House, which overlooks St Aubin's Fort, Jersey suffered extensive damage as the roof of the building was blown away.

Along the South Coast

by Fiona Baird-Murray of the Evening Argus, Brighton

IT was nearly four in the morning and, like most of Sussex, I was sound asleep.

The telephone; "Fiona, this is newsdesk. There's a bit of a gale out there and you're the only one able to reach Worthing office. We still want to piece together a paper and need early copy."

Great. Shingle from the beach 20 yards away was sharply spitting at my upstairs window. Water was seeping through the roof as tiles flew furiously about. And we had no electricity.

Outside battered beach huts huddled together, scattered yards away from their normally sunny seaside spot. A lamp-post lingered over my car — wind had already blow out its windows.

Without question Sussex had surrendered to the storm before the rest of the country. It took the full force of the 108 mph hurricane first.

My short walk to work, down the prom through the town centre and battling against the wind with every step, was terrifying.

Monstrous waves lashed against Worthing pier, suprisingly still standing. Up-turned fishing boats bounced along the beach. Windows were wrenched out of seafront shops. Brick walls had crumbled, trees lay resting, and iron railings and road signs had buckled under pressure from the elements. There was not a moving car in sight.

I ducked and dodged my way. Patrolling policemen warned of flying debris. Burglar alarm bells shrilled, breaking glass tinkled and posts swayed.

Once in the office reports flooded in about a trail of death and destruction in the wake of the hurricane across the county. Sussex was now a forest of fallen trees and smashed masonry. Roads were blocked, electricity and telephone wires had been sliced by falling trees and people everywhere were stranded — too frightened to venture out.

A man died but two others were pulled alive from tons of rubble when two storeys of the Queen's Hotel, Hastings, plummeted to the ground.

Other victims included a fisherman killed when hit by a wind-blown winch on Hastings seafront, and a mother-of-two crushed to death in her bed when a chimney stack crashed through her roof in Hove.

Two hundred caravans were flung into chaos at the Rushy Hill caravan park in Peacehaven. Pyjama-clad families dashed for safety as their homes looked like large splintered matchboxes.

In St Leonard's a three-floor terraced house caved in, and the steeple fell off St Luke's United Reform Church.

Sussex seemed secretly satisfied that it was, at least in their minds, the worst-hit county and had survived the storm.

Like any national disaster the hurricane brought with it big, warm and generous hearts. Once again people stopped in the streets and spoke to passers-by they didn't know from Adam.

One tale produced another. But the truth of the matter was that Sussex was, indeed, badly hit. Sadly there was no need to exaggerate.

At the office the phones rang and rang. Pleas for help, tales of bravado and calls for information.

In Lancing, scores of pensioners were evacuated to the parish hall when wind whipped off the roof from their sheltered housing.

In Rustington, half-constructed luxury flats collapsed like a pack of cards. There was hardly a pane of glass left in Worthing Railway station's facade, smithereens shot up to 20 yards away. Seventeen light aircraft were severely damaged at Shoreham airport.

Local landmarks did not escape the havoc. More than two thirds of the ancient Chanctonbury Ring, on the South Downs north of Worthing, were devastated. The 40 ft beech trees were planted in 1760 by 20-year-old Charles Goring who also wrote a poem about the ring. At the time there was public outcry by local people who feared the line of the South Downs would be ruined. Now it will be much missed.

The Royal Pavilion in Brighton was immediately declared out of bounds as part of a minaret, weighing two tons blasted through the roof, interrupting a £9 million restoration project.

The globe wrecked an £86,000 carpet and it took 15 men three hours to pull it out. And a huge slab of stone balanced precariously over a ceiling described as the most beautiful in Europe.

Along the coast Selsey had been described a disaster area. In the early hours desperate 999 services called on the army. Re-inforcements of more than 50 Royal Military Police were sent to the rescue. Already dozens of residents, some injured, were evacuated to Parish halls.

As if the howling winds had not been enough Sussex suffered a downpour later in the afternoon. Water poured through the gaping holes in property torn apart in the gale. Many roads were still impassable and pavements still have gigantic holes made from uprooted trees.

The dreadful scene inside the Queen's Hotel at Hastings on the day after the storm. Two storeys crashed to the ground and a man died. Two others were pulled alive from under tons of rubble.

The Rushy Hill caravan park in Peacehaven where 200 caravans were battered to pieces as pyjama-clad families dashed for safety.

*The entire roof of this six-storey apartment block at Hastings was ripped off at the height of the gale,
exposing the living accommodation below.*

Battered beach huts are scattered across the seafront at Hove. Windows in the hotels and flats on the other side of the road are smeared with salt, sand and shingle.

A tree dislodges telephone boxes outside the Pavilion Theatre, Brighton. The room on the right has an unwelcome visitor.

Photograph: Courier Newspapers

Knole House stands serenely in its park like a jewel encased in a magnificent woodland setting.
The trees in the foreground are in the gardens of Knole, a 26 acre site wholly enclosed within a high wall of Kentish ragstone.

The scene at Knole on Monday October 19, 1987. The great grave house has withstood a few gales in the past 600 years and the hurricane miraculously left it unscathed. Not so the trees in the garden and the park. Many stood for 400 years or more — to be uprooted in a single night.

Eightoaks in Kent

THE town of Sevenoaks is built on a greensand ridge that rises above the Holmesdale and Darenth Valleys and is embowered in trees. On the other side are the North Downs a solid natural escarpment that divides a collection of villages from the great wen of London. It is world of fields, forests, woods and crooked lanes and it suffered the most appalling devastation in the October storm.

Gathering information from an aerial survey and a ground inspection, the local authority estimated that the Sevenoaks area alone lost one million trees as this ruthless wind ripped its way through the countryside, inflicting damage also to thousands of homes.

Within days of the hurricane Sevenoaks was receiving international attention as the town that took the greatest impact. Six of its famous seven oaks tumbled over, there was incalculable damage to historic Knole, Chartwell, Penshurst, Hever and Ightham Mote. On television, radio, in newspapers, and in churches, homes and pubs it was talked about as the town that epitomised the experiences of thousands of people in southern England. In Jerusalem they prayed for Sevenoaks.

Even before the army had finished cutting their way through the mass of fallen trees, an appeal launched by Sevenoaks District Council had raised more than £75,000. On December 6, on the famous Vine Cricket ground, Sevenoaks staged a Hurricane Fayre and replaced the stricken oaks with seven saplings.

On the day of the Hurricane Fayre, Gloria Hunniford, radio and television personality, and her daughter, Blue Peter presenter Caron Keating and others representing the business life of the community were invited to plant seven saplings. As Sevenoaks came under the national spotlights again, more than 5,000 people were there to jostle with television crews.

On the first anniversary of the Great Storm, the seven oak saplings were vandalised and the town again became the focus of attention all over the world. The trunks of two of the trees had been split lengthways, leaving just a splintered stump. The others had been snapped in half, the top branches lurching at an angle.

A ceremony to bury a time capsule containing newspapers, tapes and books recording the destruction wrought in that one night in 1987 went ahead despite the vandalism, but the poignancy of the ceremony was felt by all present. As Sevenoaks again made preparations to replace their oak trees, Prince Charles spoke of his sadness and a national newspaper offered £1,000 reward for information leading to conviction of the culprits.

Has someone spilled a box of matches and left them higgledy piggledy on the ground? Closer examination will show these are fallen firs near Westerham, Kent. The hurricane has opened up great new vistas and for those who know this area it will take many months to become accustomed to what is now unfamiliar territory.

It is normal for motorists travelling down Toys Hill to beware at this stage. There is a steep hill,
the road narrows and crossroads appear after a sharp bend. There were no cars on the morning of Sunday October 18
when David Court took this picture — just mile upon mile of fallen trees.

Photograph: Courier Newspapers

Foxwold, Brasted Chart, Kent is the family home of Jack and Diana Pym and was built by Mr Pym's grandfather Horace 103 years ago in a woodland setting. The house gained considerable fame last year when it was used by film makers Merchant and Ivory for their award-winning film Room with a View. Today the house has a changed view of its own, across the North Downs, to where the formerly smooth capped curve of Polhill now wears a spiked hair cut.

A Sussex woodland north of Brighton. Upside down trees and vast roots litter the ground.

Photograph: Courier Newspapers

Pickmoss, a 500 year-old house in Otford High Street Kent was severely damaged when a Scots pine crashed onto the roof of the building. The owner of the house, Jennifer Firbank was shaken by the ordeal but uninjured. The tree knocked a massive hole in the side of the house and had to be lifted clear by a giant crane after a tree feller perched high above the village of Otford had abseiled to the tree top with his chainsaw. Pictures show the tree and house before and after.

Farm buildings at Fir Tree House, Chart Sutton near Ashford were brought crashing to the ground. It certainly looks as if a hurricane has passed this way.

Tempest of 1703

THE most destructive storm ever known in the history of the British Isles came on the night of November 26, 1703 when hurricane force winds which had moved upwards from the southern hemisphere flattened everything in its terrifying path south of a line from Bristol to London.

The Great Storm as history has described it killed people, uprooted trees in their thousands, blew roofs off houses, destroyed precious windmills and ripped lead linings off churches and rolled them up like paper.

Throughout the country people and animals, caught in the open, were blown off their feet. Terrified birds were pulled from the sky and those inside insecure homes rushed out into the street, only to be hit by falling masonry or flying tiles and slates.

The Eddystone Lighthouse was a victim of the storm. Henry Winstanley, the builder, was actually in the lighthouse conducting repairs when it was swept off the Eddystone Reef and crushed into a thousand pieces on the rocks below.

The 1703 tempest reached its peak towards midnight and continued to around six o'clock the next morning. Daniel Defoe wrote that no pen could describe it, nor tongue express it nor thought conceive it unless by one who was in the extremity of it.

For two weeks previous to its dreadful climax winds had been blowing across southern England and up the English Channel when, in a series of Atlantic depressions, gale followed gale. It started in the south-west and increased to such tremendous violence that the storm that followed was like a gigantic air raid, the damage almost cosmic in scale.

At its height the wind roared like thunder and the tales of the night read more like an adventure story than a narrative of fact. For example.

○ At St Peter's in Thanet a cow was found still alive in the uppermost branches of a tree.

○ From Sandwich to Canterbury river banks were littered with fish blown out of the River Stour.

○ Near Faversham in Kent the London-Dover mail coach was blown by a gust of wind a distance of 30 feet and landed upturned in a ditch, its occupants unharmed.

○ The church steeple at Brenchley was the tallest in Kent until it crashed across its cloisters.

○ On the River Severn a tidal wave swept upwards and drowned an estimated 15,000 sheep.

○ In London Queen Anne took refuge in the palace cellar as masonry crashed through the roof.

○ The area surrounding the North Foreland lighthouse was showered with hot cinders blown from the open coal fire on its summit, spreading fire to thatched buildings for miles around.

○ As far inland as Cranbrook, grazing land was rendered useless by salt spray blown 25 miles from the sea.

○ The Bishop of Bath and his wife were both killed when a chimney stack collapsed on the bedroom.

Although only 19 people died in the hurricane of 1987 compared with the thousands who perished in 1703, the two great storms have many parallels. Defoe wrote that many people listening to the wind believed it was the end of the world. Similar thoughts accompanied those lying terrified in their beds 250 years later — and it didn't only apply, as Defoe suggested, to the simple minded.

Another similarity was in the sudden increased cost of building repairs. In 1703 roofing tiles went up from 21s to £6 per 1,000 and a bricklayer's wages from 2s to 5s a day.

The big difference was the effect of the storm at sea. Thousands of seamen perished in The Great Storm and the Royal Navy, with its heavily manned ships, lost an entire fleet. It was the worst disaster in naval history especially for the warships of the ill-fated Channel Squadron which were battered to pieces on the Goodwin Sands.

The death toll reads as follows: Flagship *Mary*, 272 men and 60 guns; *Restoration*, 386 men; *Northumberland* 253 men; *Stirling Castle*, 279 men and all 70 guns.

After this tragedy all the flags in England were flying at half mast and even the Queen wore mourning. On the Goodwin Sands there was nothing to mark the spot where England's pride has sunk for ever.

Other warships lost included the bomb ketch, *Portsmouth* at the Nave, the 50 gun *Reserve* at Yarmouth, the storeship *Canterbury* at Bristol, the *Newcastle* at Chichester. The 50 gun *Vigo* and the bomb ketch *Motar* were driven ashore on the Dutch coast. The 70 gun *Resolution* and advice boat *Eagle* were beached in shallow water without loss.

The Great Storm of 1703 was a tragedy for the Royal Navy and on land it caused vast destruction. For the details of this tempest we have to thank the diligent journalist, Daniel Defoe who carried out a nation wide investigation before publishing his informative report.

Photograph: Isle of Thanet Gazette

A gaping hole in the roof. Men perched precariously on splintered timbers. A doomed tree in the foreground. This was the scene at Queen's Avenue, Westgate, Kent — a sight repeated all over southern England.

Photograph: Isle of Thanet Gazette

Farmer, Edward Spanton of Minster whose house was surrounded by fir trees had a lucky escape when eleven 100-year-old trees fell in an hour — all of them just missing his house.

There was a tree on a house in almost every community in southern England. This one was at Oxted. close to the Kent and Surrey border.

Photograph: Isle of Thanet Gazette

Nursing sister Bridget Kelly, Sister Rose, and Sister Superior Joseph at Bon Secours Nursing Home, Ramsgate survey the scene where a giant cedar, believed to be 400 years old, crashed to the ground.

High sided vehicles were totally exposed to nature's wrath. This one near Gravesend was an early victim.

The spire of the Clock Tower of the former Lawn Road primary school in Northfleet, Kent was snapped off. Two firemen lowered it to safety and to add insult to injury thieves later stole much of the valuable lead casing.

Photograph: Kentish Times

Weekend groceries are a necessity whatever the conditions.
Two housewives at Chatham thread themselves and their baskets through fallen giants.

Photograph: Kent Messenger

Garden centres which had taken a heavy battering in January's blizzard suffered again as the winds tore them to shreds. Here, nurserymen Peter McBride (left) and Peter Clark of Pete's Nursery, Hawkhurst embark on the weary task of picking up the pieces.

Photograph: Kent Messenger

John Munn at Spills Hill, farm, Staplehurst lost half his apple trees in the storm, Arable crops were also scorched probably by salt blown in from the sea. Mr Munn is pictured here with Maidstone MP Ann Widdecombe. For fruit farmers the situation was desperate.

49

The giant cedar fell at Standen House, near East Grinstead. The residents here were cut off for five weeks by fallen trees.

50

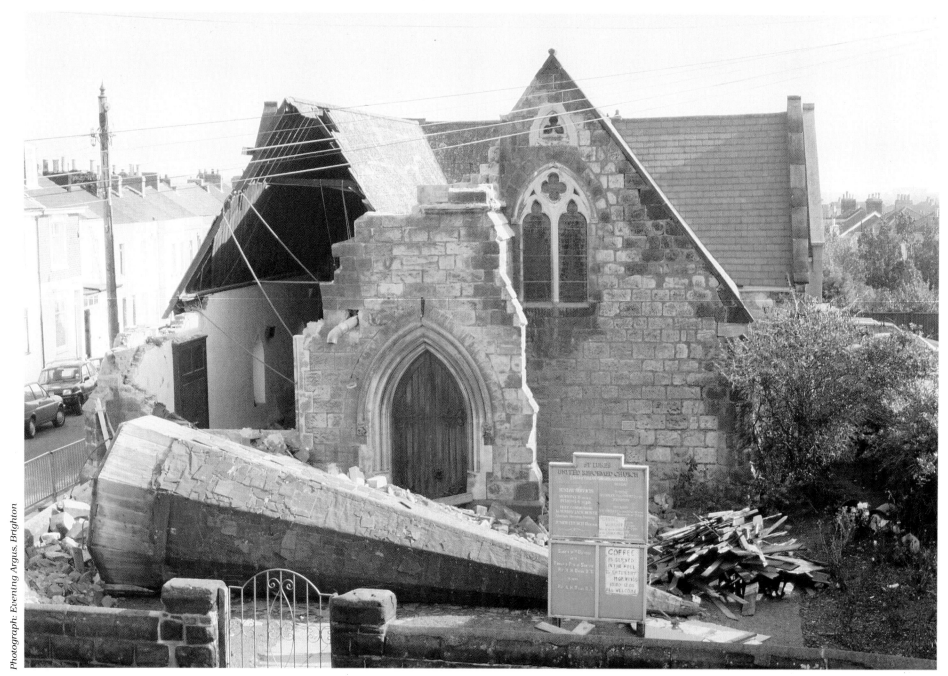

St. Luke's United Reformed Church, St. Leonard's, Sussex.

Noble Tree Road, Hildenborough — the picture that says it all.

The root of this tree opened a large crater on the footpath of Mote Road, Maidstone. A passing cyclist surveys the damage.

53

Sevenoaks Vine cricket ground, with pavilion in the background, seen through the branches of one of the six fallen oak trees.

Toys Hill woodlands, the birthplace of the National Trust, was the site of the greatest destruction, losing 99% of its trees.

Rochester City Council leader Doug McInnes and city services manager, David Newell at The Vines, Rochester,
Their problem is pretty daunting.

The damage at Kew Gardens included the loss of many rare specimens including this huge Tree of Heaven — AILANTHUS ALTISSIMA which fell appropriately enough on the roof of King William's Temple built in 1837.

Photograph: Mark Marques, National Trust

Wakehurst Place, the country garden for Kew suffered with the loss of 55 per cent of their exotic trees but the recovery has been amazing. As a result of good management there is a 20-year-old arboretum waiting to take over. Tony Schilling, the curator is optimistic and stresses the importance of variety in the age and type of tree planted to protect against disasters.

The rhododendron walk at Wakehurst Place was completely destroyed but an entirely new Asian heath garden has been planted to suit the light now coming in.

The Royal Horticultural Society gardens at Wisley also recovered well in spite of losing many valuable specimens. On the left is a toppled eucalyptus dalrympleana and on the right many fallen pines obscure a path at Battleston Hill.

Photograph: Heather Angel

61

The view from the air showing the damage at Petworth Park in Sussex after the storm.

Photograph: Mike Howarth, National Trust

One of the most fascinating results of the storm was the revelation of archaeological remains at Highdown Hill near Worthing in Sussex. On the site of an Anglo-Saxon burial ground and Bronze Age settlement, a grove of trees blew down holding bones in their roots. An eleven week dig led by Mark Gardiner of the Institute of Archaeology, took place in the summer of 1988 and many interesting finds were recorded.

Photograph: Les Hunt

Motorists who drive along the road between Ide Hill and Sevenoaks stop and stare in disbelief. Nature's power has punched great gaps in the hillside, revealing breathtaking views across the Weald of Kent. The trees which remain are garlanded with frills of young leaves.

Surrey

FOR fashionable Surrey, with its stockbroker belt of elegant houses, thickly wooded forests and charts and commuter towns, there was no respite. Reaching the county by 1.30 am, at 3.30 the storm was at its zenith, the barometric pressure at its lowest, the howling roaring winds at their most frightening.

Limpsfield Chart, Reigate Hill and the whole length of The North Downs and Greensand Ridge were hacked to pieces. Giant trees lay against giant trees by the side of the hills, across the roads, on top of houses, churches and schools. At first light police ordered Surrey not to move; with few roads open and trains not running it couldn't. As isolation hit Surrey the city was also at a standstill. The next big crash was not far away.

A home for elderly ladies at Blindley Heath was so badly damaged by falling chimneys that its residents had to be evacuated to the church hall; the Red Cross hall at Oxted was totally demolished and in The Purley Way a 60 year old disabled woman died of fright, her pet dog pining by her side.

During the night distress calls came to Surrey fire brigade at the rate of one call every 30 seconds. Chimney pots tumbled at the Old Ship pub at Tatsfield; a fireman was injured as he attended an electricity sub-station in Dorking and in the same town an ambulance crew and their patient had a terrifying journey as trees fell all around them on their way to Crawley hospital; at one point the ambulancemen had to cut through a fallen tree but as they did two more fell just a few feet in front. They abandoned the vehicle and sought shelter in a nearby house.

Weathermen had predicted the storm would miss mainland Britain, but at Box Hill Nora Bale's three dogs gave every sign that they were aware of the impending disaster; on Thursday they ran from home to garden all evening whimpering incessantly. Their instinct proved correct; the mobile home where Mr and Mrs Bale lived began to rock and sway terrifyingly and trees flew past like matchsticks. All the couple could do was pray together until the hurricane passed.

For the East Surrey Water Company it was the wettest October of the century and the River Mole was on Flood alert posing a further threat to Leigh, Brockham and Leatherhead.

In Surrey as in Sussex and Kent many famous beauty spots suffered grievously. The famous Clandon beeches were severely reduced. Wakehurst Place at Ardingley (the country nursery of Kew Gardens) lost 50% of its oak trees and Godstone Green lost half its conker trees.

Photograph: Sean Brown

Peter Clifford at Chart Way, Reigate (far right) slept through the storm until a fir tree rudely interrupted his slumbers at 5 am. The tree crashed through the roof damaging two bedrooms.

Trailing wires and fallen trees at Waller lane, Caterham fail to worry the ramblers. Somehow the lamp post survived.

Photograph: Surrey Mirror

The couple who live in Honeycrock Court, Salfords, Surrey were asleep when this 70 ft tree fell. Terry and Gail Richmond thought a bomb had dropped on their flat.

The Royal dilemma

Dr Brinsley Burbridge (*pictured right*) a senior member at the Royal Botanic Gardens at Kew climbs over the remains of a 200-year-old oak tree which toppled in front of the Palm House where tropical plants are grown.

The damage at Kew caused a considerable impact on the nation. Not only because more than 1,000 trees were destroyed or badly damaged but many valuable specimens were lost.

Among the casualities are the oldest recorded specimen of *Zelkova Carpinifolia* which dates from 1761, three *Nothofagus Obliqua*, 80 foot tall and dating from 1902 and one of only two *Himalayan* elms in the country.

The landscape at Kew has radically altered. Seven out of the ten trees which lined the Broad Walk have gone and the curators will need every penny of the grants which have been made available by the Government for the restoration of historic parks.

As more and more standing trees are felled because of their dangerous condition or unsightly look, the toll in London's royal parks is increasing. Hyde Park has lost more than 300 trees, Richmond Park 100 and well over 1000 have gone in the grounds of Hampton Court Palace.

Before the storm London received more than 4in of rain and the ground turned to a soggy mess. When the wind blew, the great broad-leaved giants were upended. Their loss is grievous.

Photograph: Press Association

This could be described as a trunk call. An uprooted tree crashed on to the kiosk outside the Victoria and Albert museum.

69

That wartime spirit of camaraderie applied not only to those who live in the countryside or smaller towns. People in central London rarely meet their neighbours but lasting friendships were made during the eventful weekend which followed the storm. Here the residents of Eccleston Square, Pimlico take a break from cleaning up with a picnic in the park.

Sadly, a man died when his car was hit by a falling tree on the Petersfield to Chichester Road in Hampshire.
Firemen work to release the Ford Capri from beneath the tree.

Hampshire and the Isle of Wight

NATURE'S wrath unleashed itself on the Isle of Wight early on the Friday morning and such was the impact of the wind and the noise of the night many people thought the island itself might be carried away by the storm.

First light revealed all. The heaving, surging tides were still those of Southampton Waters and the English Channel but the land had been bulldozed and stripped and almost defied description.

Generations to come will talk about the night of October 16, 1987 and how the jaws of the hurricane closed its awesome teeth over Wight, felling homes and trees, blowing caravans to pieces, wrecking seafront arcades and even chopping Shanklin's famous Victorian pier in half.

On the mainland it was the same story. Over interminable miles seafront paraphernalia was reduced to a sagging pile of debris. Having battered the Isle of Wight it roared up the Solent, hit Southampton, Portsmouth and Southsea below the belt and then took a destructive path into the Hampshire countryside.

Boats in Portchester harbour were tossed around like discarded toys, Mature trees entrenched beneath pavements were uprooted in Gosport, Nurseries and farm buildings collapsed. Scaffolding at Southsea flew in the air like arrows and speared a nearby car.

The wind circled around the big wheel at Beachlands, Hayling Island, wrapped it up in a tangled, twisted ball of metal and took it for a ride around the grounds of the funfair. A gable end crashed through the roof of a motor cycle centre in Portsmouth and damaged scores of machines. Cars were buried in every town and the Parade Hotel at Southsea took an unprecedented battering. Glasshouses disintegrated, a horticulturist at Warsash losing £42,000 worth of polythene tunnels, 65,000 cyclamen plants and 3,000 panes of glass. Throughout Hampshire garden centres faced losses running into hundreds of thousands of pounds.

The once heavily tree-lined A3 main road to London was closed after the storm, and trains did not run until the Sunday. Calls for help began at 2 am and Hampshire Fire Brigade had answered 4,000 by the following Tuesday. At Petersfield they had to free the body of a motorist killed by a falling tree.

In the southern electricity area half a million customers were without power, 110,000 in the Solent division and 100,000 in Test covering parts of West Sussex and the rest of Hampshire. The county police received 1,600 999 calls in 24 hours after the storm — and every one was an emergency.

Photograph: The News, Portsmouth

Fallsbrook Nursery, Sidlesham, Hampshire needed a little attention after being ravaged by the storm. Here, two assistants salvage frames and glass.

*The force of the wind turned this mobile home on to its roof at the
Harbour site, Portsmouth.*

Three Days in October

The Fox and Hounds at Toys Hill near Westerham is close to the Kent and Surrey border and, at 800 feet, one of the highest pubs in southern England. The well and terrace at Toys Hill were given by the co-founder of the National Trust, Octavia Hill and the dense woodlands around bear her name today. Hazel Pelling, the landlady of the Fox and Hounds keeps a diary and these are the events as she recorded them during the three days after the storm.

FRIDAY OCTOBER 16

IN the night Toys Hill was transformed from the magical woods that would soon be gold, and later, great vaulted cathedrals of snow and ice — back to windswept, near treeless uplands of the turn of the century.

We got up this morning and for the first time, could see dawn from our garden. During the night the Toys Hill woods had vanished, redeployed in a great God-laid parquet floor over the leaves.

From every approaching lane, we had been penned in by impenetrable stockades. Quickly organising indomitable working teams, local residents began to clear up, and work their way out.

At the Fox and Hounds, the floor was sawdust, end to end — torches of every sort and flamboyant headgear all along the counters. Every hand that lifted a pint was grimed from manual exertion and from crawling through undergrowth. Every new arrival, commando streaked and leaf decorated, got a cheer. Mick Howard played: "If you go down in the woods today" and "Whistle while you work".

Everyone has been out on the road to share experiences, to discuss manoeuvres and meet neighbours never before known. We crawled through a tunnel of fallen pine, scratching the ground underneath from time to time; if there was tarmac underneath we were going in the right direction. As we pushed forward the scent of crushed pine alternated with the scents of crushed beechleaf.

Whilst scrambling through branches, hauling ourselves up and over, forced into detours, suddenly other heads would pop through the branches — or legs — or dangling feet to be followed by a body, Robin Hood like, swinging to the ground. We all look around — discuss the best way forward or back. It is like a jungle encounter in a B-movie where Kentish Hills are being substituted for the tangled vegetation of Malaya.

What would a stranger make of the steady stream of adults in and out of one particular garage on Toys Hill? That car-phone was the only link with the outside world.

SATURDAY OCTOBER 17

Torrential rain for a short spell, makes walking even more difficult on the mud and leaves, tree trunks and branches. But we collect eight gallons of water in buckets under the leaking gutters. We have no piped water and no cooking facilities because we have had to put out the Aga. We do not like the new, unfamiliar cold kitchen. Smokey-log toast and savoury mince warmed over the open fire, make a delicious meal.

The chorus of saws never stops all day.

Clare Jarvis motors down from college in Cambridge. Turns up Chart lane and her car meets a tree. She has to leave it in Brasted and continue in the gathering dusk, with no torch. She struggled through the massed timber till, exhausted, she sees the home of friends at the top of the Chart. Here she is given a candle-lit supper and then escorted, as if in a resistance escape line, up to the Fox and Hounds.

Here everyone exchanges stories and later Clare joins a dozen or so friends and neighbours making for the Toys Hill crossroads. In a line they climb trees and fall down slides of massed branches, slip, slither and haul and squirm downwards. Clare arrives on the family doorstep towards midnight. Her elegant white coat is black and green, her hair full of twigs and leaves. "I do so hope our lovely willow is still by the pond" she says. But it's not.

SUNDAY OCTOBER 18

The contractors who "broke through" on Toys Hill did so with breath-taking efficiency and determination. The monster JCB gobbled up tree trunks and tossed them aside quite flippantly. Totally camouflaged one moment behind a towering mountain of branches and leaves, the next we saw a yellow flash — then a waving excavator bucket. Relentlessly the machine came forward, backwards, sideways, forward, reverse, shove, backwards, reverse, push, shove, batter. Eventually it made the final obstructions and emerged, triumphant, followed by army vehicles which had arrived too late to help on this stretch. They moved round to the Care Village approaches.

All the hill was out this afternoon to assess and digest the final devastation, and to marvel at the sudden views across to Ide Hill and beyond to Ashdown Forest.

The road is one track; the white lines are obscured with leaves. Our road has become a Victorian woodland track once more.

We have slipped back to the landscape of 80 or more years ago and a lifestyle to match. Candlepower and water collection, of communication by personal visit or letter, rural timbering pursuits, house mending and patching, walks and early nights.

"Your father and I played Patience last night" said Eileen to her astonished daughter Alicia. "I think you and father have made more conversation during these three days, than you have in a year" said Alicia.

Power technicians, communications experts, foresters, builders, plumbers and good neighbours everywhere are working, like surgeons in other disasters, to restore life and rehabilitate a great stretch of rural England.

Geordie Prest, the Toys Hill warden for the National Trust, sees all his many years' work erased. With touching optimism he says: "I went out yesterday to see where we could mark out new walks for the future."

Photograph: David Sache

Damage at Sheffield Park, Sussex.

Photograph: Jon Rodwell

The Fox and Hounds pub at Toys Hill.

Not many trees down but acres of flooded fields. This was Tonbridge two days after the storm.

Three days after the gale hit southern England, west Wales suffered its own tragedy when the front carriage of the 5.20 am train from Swansea to Shrewsbury plunged into the river Towy near Glanrhyd. This dramatic aerial view shows the remains of the bridge in waters swollen by many days of incessant rain.

Some famous storms

February 1953: A deep depression moved east-north-east from south of Iceland and then turned rapidly south-east into the North Sea, while pressure rose rapidly in the west, producing a steep pressure gradient. In south England the gales were accompanied by heavy driving rain and low cloud. In the north channel the motor vessel Princess Victoria sank with the loss of 132 lives. At Kings Lynn the predicted tide was 6.6 metres (21.6 feet) but the water came up 2.5 metres (8.2 feet) higher. The town centre was flooded by a wave. No one knew the flood water was coming as the noise it made was muffled by the roaring gale. At Sheerness the peak tide was 2.1 metres higher than expected. 20 people were trapped in a coach between Sittingbourne and Sheerness and had to be rescued the next morning by an amphibious vehicle. On the Essex shore, most of Canvey Island's 12,000 people were taken elsewhere to safety. 156 people lost their lives in the four counties of Lincolnshire, Norfolk, Suffolk and Essex.

February 1962: On Feburary 11 a deep depression moved rapidly south-east towards southern Norway bringing severe gales to Scotland and Northern Ireland. Wind speed in Lanarkshire was measured at 123 mph. In Sheffield the maximum gust was 96 mph. More than 7,000 houses were damaged, three people were killed and about 250 injured. At Southwold on the Suffolk coast where a number of people lost their lives in 1953, the sea reached the high water mark at low tide. The storm surge passed when the time came for normal high tide. Conditions were not so bad as they had been in 1953 because the surge and the high tide did not coincide.

January 1976: After almost a week of stormy weather a depression moved across Scotland into the North Sea during the night of January 2/3, subsequently deepening and bringing severe gales with winds of hurricane force or more. Among high gusts were 105 mph at Wittering, 108 mph at Cromer, 102 mph at Norwich, 76 mph at Holborn, London. Norwich was badly hit. At 11.0 that night every road out of the city was blocked by fallen trees. In the city itself 600 trees were blown down and many houses damaged. Structural damage was widespread in nearly every county but it was most severe in a wide band from Northern Ireland across Lancashire and the Midlands to East Anglia. British Rail services were severely disrupted by fallen power lines and trees on the track. At Liverpool a newly built ferry was sunk and damage over the country was estimated at as much £100 million. The storm was considered to be as bad as Defoe's 1703 tempest.

Generally the sky was very clear with only broken fast-moving clouds. But there were continual flashes, not of lightning as many supposed at the time, but caused by the thrashing and short-circuiting of high tension cables by branches.

As with the storms of 1953 and 1962 the depression produced a storm-surge in the North Sea but the improved sea defences were only breached in a few places notably at Cleethorpes where more than 100 homes had to be evacuated.

24 people died in Britain mainly from falling trees and road accidents attributed to storm damage.

January 10-11, 1978: A rapidly deepening depression moved across England towards the Netherlands and severe northerly gales developed behind it. The London weather centre recorded gusts of 81 mph and numerous roads were blocked by fallen trees. Round the coast the piers at Margate, Herne Bay, Hunstanton and Skegness were either badly damaged or destroyed.

Dame Jennifer Jenkins (left), chairman of the National Trust and Lady Neville at Emmetts, Ide Hill.

Photograph: Evening Echo, Basildon

On January 31, 1953, a storm surge driven by ferocious north-westerly winds crashed against the east coast sea defences.
The damage extended more than a 1,000 miles and 307 people died.
In Canvey Island, Essex, where these young people are wading in flood waters, 13,000 were evacuated.

Margate pier, which was due for demolition, was smashed to pieces in the gale which moved across England on January 10, 1978.

The torrential rain of furious intensity which lashed Kent for two days in September 1968 caused untold damage in the Thames, Medway, Eden and Darenth Valleys. This was the scene at Chipstead when the waters had subsided.

The National Trust

by Arland Kingston

THE National Trust, along with thousands of other landowners and tenants, has suffered a complete change to its properties in the south-east of England as a result of the hurricane of 16 October 1987. The catalogue of damage is far too widespread to detail, and the distress the destruction has caused to those closely involved in the countryside has been frightful. We must not, however, dwell on the past. What has happened has happened and our duty is now to work towards the future and face what is proving to be an unequalled challenge and a great opportunity to replace and replant.

After the hurricane the immediate need was to attend to public safety, and this, together with opening up the roadways and tracks, removing trees from buildings and dealing with the many small crises, diverted everyone's attention from the sheer horror of the destruction and it brought out a marvellous 'wartime' type of spirit in us all. Help was offered and accepted from other parts of the country and volunteers of all types came forward to do their bit. Despite help the cost of this phase for private and public landowners has been high and little money has been made available from the public purse.

The next stage has been the hard, dangerous work of systematically clearing up the mess. This is a job for professionals and very little outside help can be given. In some of the larger show gardens such as Sheffield Park and the private garden of Leonardslee more than 2,000 trees came down. As a single large tree can take a gang of men up to a week to dispose of, the measure of the cost can be assessed. Some properties are easier to clear than others depending on the density of the tree destruction, but the complete flattening of the woods along the greensand ridge to the west of Sevenoaks presents the woodland gangs with a nightmare. This clearance will take years to complete in some cases but it must be done to enable the woodland areas to come back to life again and regeneration or planting to take hold and replace that which we have lost.

While doing the clearance work we must be mindful of the natural history interest and the need to leave certain areas wild and others with fallen trunks and branches to take the smaller species into the future. The clinical clearance of the countryside could now do as much damage as the hurricane itself.

The process is time consuming and everyone needs patience. The money needed to complete the first phases of the work will regulate progress as well as the availability of skilled staff. It is only when all this has been done that we can consider planting again and the planning will be vital if we are going to pass on to our successors woods, parks and gardens of which we can be proud so that they can enjoy their beauty.

The gardens have been damaged but they remain beautiful. People who know them well will be saddened by the loss of so many old friends but the loss of these trees has opened up new views, new areas can be planted and will become fresh features in the gardens. In the parkland the problem of under planting shelter belts, clumps and shaws has been lessened by the heavy thinning of the trees which will enable light to get in for the new young plants to establish themselves and thrive. The replacements will have a better chance and will be more faithful than the original planting of the park.

In the woodlands we must encourage the natural regeneration which will usually spring up to replace a major loss such as this, but if fresh planting does take place then we must be careful to put in compatible species and replace like with like. It is time to redress the wrongs of the past where some of the black coniferous areas have been destroyed and will be replaced with a mixture which will please nature as well as our own eyes.

The damage has been disastrous, the cost of rehabilitation will be frighteningly high, but the hope for the future is strong and now that we are beginning to see where we are going there is a tremendous feeling of enthusiasm among all those involved.

TO fund the restoration work, The National Trust is appealing for donations which should be sent to:

The National Trust Trees and Gardens
Storm Disaster Appeal
PO Box 39
Bromley
Kent BR1 1NH
Telephone: 01-464 1111 *for credit card contributions.*

Photograph: National Trust

Scotney Castle Garden, Lamberhurst, Kent before the recovery

Bateman's, the former home of Rudyard Kipling, features a lily pond, formal lawn, orchard garden and numerous fallen trees, including the one in this picture which Kipling planted early this century.

The serene tranquility of Scotney Castle remains despite the chaos of the storm.

Sheffield Park Gardens, Sussex.

Octavia Hill Woods, Toys Hill, Kent.

Felbrigg Hall in Norfolk

Nymans Gardens, Sussex. The Summer House.

Chartwell, Kent. The view east from the terrace.

Petworth, Sussex.

91

Emmetts House and Garden, Ide Hill, Kent. Beech Lodge (top right) was cut off with Care Village for many days, making headline news.

The face of Reigate Hill was changed forever as hundreds of grand old trees yielded to the wind's power.

93

Bodiam Castle. The dead and wounded lie all around.

Taken from the roof of Emmetts House, Ide Hill, Kent Michael Knights' dramatic picture shows the new view of the North Downs from the Darent Valley to the Medway Gap.

The North Downs Way a long-distance footpath which runs from Farnham to Dover is one of the most heavily wooded areas in the south-east. In this picture walkers find their way impeded by fallen giants at Reigate Hill, Surrey.
This part of the chalk downs in Surrey is owned by the National Trust.

The Eastern Counties

AS the storm swept north and east, Southend, with its south-facing coastline was one of the first Essex towns to feel the onslaught of the wind. The morning revealed a scene of dreadful chaos with lorries overturned, shop fronts smashed and roofs ripped open. As if a giant beast had gone beserk, the roads were littered with glass, slates, kiosks, beach huts, shelters and even boats.

The most amazing effect of the wind's strength was that it held back the oncoming tide. Like Moses and the Red Sea it was possible to walk across the mud to the Pierhead at high tide. The Wallasea Marina with 60 wrecked boats in tow was swept across the River Crouch to Burnham; at Southend airport a hugh hangar collapsed and Norsey Woods, the pride of Basildon, were massacred.

Miraculously only one life was lost, despite the suicidal attempts of sailboard enthusiasts who attempted to venture forth into the 70 mph winds on Friday morning.

All along the coast from Leigh to Shoeburyness boats were lifted from the sea by the wind and dumped on to dry land with hundreds of craft completely wrecked.

In mid-Suffolk, Stowmarket was devastated. The River Rod burst its banks and Sudbury, together with many villages, was cut off. A newly-built Methodist chapel in Trimley-St-Martin collapsed. The Earl William, known as the "prison ship" housing Tamil refugees, broke its moorings and drifted into the Stour estuary where it ran aground.

In Ipswich, as elsewhere, the damage to property was enormous. Lorries were overturned on the Orwell Bridge as drivers ignored warnings to avoid the crossing. At Felixstowe a major disaster was narrowly averted at the docks. The Silver Falcon carrying a toxic cargo was severely holed when it broke loose and crashed into an oil jetty. The dock police sealed the port at 4.30 am, and thousands of people were evacuated from the area.

Within five miles of the sea the forests of Rendlesham and Tunstall were 80 per cent razed and the nearby town of Woodbridge described by the police as "a mess".

In Norfolk, Norwich mourned the loss of hundreds of fine trees. At Pulham Market, Tyrells Wood, saved two years previously by the Woodland Trust, suffered immeasurable damage. As with the rest of the country the mature and handsome trees fell leaving behind the saplings that bent with the wind.

Photograph: East Anglian Daily Times

Co-op milkman, Keith Joy, on his way to Brantham, had a miraculous escape when two large fir trees fell in front of his delivery vehicle. He went for help and on his return found the lorry smashed and buried beneath another tree.

On the sign:

↑ Chelmsford
A131

Bury
St. Edmunds
A131 (A134) →

↑ Bulmer Road
Industrial Estate

Stour Street, Sudbury became a pedestrianised area as trees sealed off the town centre.

Photograph: East Anglian Times

Roofs were ripped off these flat-roofed houses in Annbrook Road on the Belstead estate, Ipswich, exposing them to the elements. Parked cars are damaged by flying debris.

Photograph: East Anglian Times

The owner of this car stopped in Stoke Park Drive, Ipswich to get help after a fallen tree blocked his route. He returned to find the car flattened.

Photograph: Eastern Daily Press

A Norwich businessman ponders an uncertain future after his factory was wrecked by the storm. David Davenport soon moved his business to his Thorpe home.

Farm buildings took a terrible battering in the gale. Here Michael Maguire of Beccles sits among the rubble that was once his barn.

Two 13-year-old boys, Simon Davies (left) and Andy Fry with the crushed car they discovered at Thetford.

View from the Air

By Fiona MacLeod

ON the Monday after the hurricane we flew over much of the worst-hit area of West Kent to take some aerial photographs. It was a clear, sharp but still autumn day and the sun shone.

From the air perspective and proportion become distorted. The picture is wider but the living detail — the twisted branches and scarred earth — is lost. So much of the wooded high ground of Brasted Chart, Toys Hill and Ide Hill, felled in great random swathes, resembled nothing more dramatic than an abandoned game of spillikins.

In contrast elsewhere there was a bizarre orderliness in the lengths of road-side trees which had all fallen in the same way, domino-like — further evidence of the night's destructive game playing.

The furious character of the hurricane had altered some areas beyond recognition and yet from above I could also see neat fields, hedges and solitary oaks untouched.

We flew from Biggin Hill airfield, south over Brasted Chart towards Bough Beech, circling often and dipping to 600 feet to find the best angles on what were some of the worst stretches of sheer scale destruction in the whole one and half hour flight.

Substantial houses, screened from passers-by with woodland, planned with skill and grown to maturity in previous generations, seemed bare and vulnerable as they rose from the battered and flattened trees.

Towards Edenbridge the floods obscured much of surrounding lanes and fields. It was not until we turned north and flew over Sevenoaks that individual scenes leapt up from the ground and became for me the most telling symbols of the hurricane.

Sevenoaks Vine, where five of its oaks lay fanned outwards from the pitch, each with a blood-clot of earth and root open to the sky above a deep brown scar in the circle of green. The sixth fallen tree was already a pale yellow blur of sawdust, wood slivers and new logs. Small clumps of colour studded the scene; children climbing the trunks, parents taking photographs, people simply standing to stare.

The garden entrails of two rows of large houses backing onto each other, which I could not identify, spilling out into a wide splash of branch and tree-trunk, crossing and re-crossing, smashing into neat hedges and tidy lawns.

Riverhill, the three-lane main road unrecognisable as a winding, light-coloured track disappearing into Amazon jungle.

And the one image which stayed in my mind long after the plane had landed was of the small valley in Knole Park. As we flew along its length, not a tree remained standing. All those that were felled lay in straight lines, stripped of smaller branches and foliage. One or two stumps rose up towards us and a footpath, newly open to the skies, cut a line like a knife through this battlefield full of the dead.

Our Darkest Hours

AS Southern England was plunged into total darkness, the biggest emergency operation since the second world war swung dramatically into action. It began at daybreak on Black Friday and continued relentlessly for almost a month. It involved many thousands of men, some tragically losing their lives. And it proved just how dependent we are on the great energy of electricity.

The battle to restore power started almost as soon as the first desperate calls came into Electricity Board offices in dozens of centres. A message from the Central Electricity Generating Board triggered the call-out system. An unbelievable drop in power, showing that lines were toppling down, was accurately monitored and an umbrella system of contacts spread the news throughout the country.

At first only the regular staff were involved but as the emergency calls flooded in at a horrific rate it soon became clear that a countrywide task force would have to be drafted in.

Eastern Electricity Board crews were joined by repair teams from London, the Midlands, north-west England, Yorkshire and Merseyside. Seeboard's great rescue army arrived by van, train and plane from places as far away as Scotland, Wales and Ireland. Southern recruited 700 including many from Ulster.

All of them were overwhelmed by the devastation they found. Even those from the Scottish Highlands who had seen some of the worst weather conditions in Britain were shocked by the scale of the damage which confronted them. Overhead power lines lay in tangled coils across hundreds of miles of country lanes. Poles were smashed like matchwood. Transformers were uprooted and underground cables severed as the trees toppled like ninepins. Conductors were pinned to the ground under the great, rain-soaked weight of dying hardwood. Insulators lay smashed and sub-station fences were blown to smithereens.

Householders had to survive without electricity for several days, and in some cases weeks, and the amount of rotting food thrown out from freezers will never be known. Some people travelled miles for a bath and modern technology ground to a halt, making it forcibly apparent how much we have come to depend on this great essential power.

Engineers and linesmen from other areas came with barely a change of clothes or much money in their pockets as they thought they would be needed for just a day or two. For up to 16 days the men toiled. Separated from their wives they slept as little as five hours a night and in some cases went many days without a bath.

Assisted by the army this great and growing team of skilled engineers were winning their battle and in streets throughout southern England lights suddenly shone again. The really gruelling work then began of fighting through the most rural, heavily-wooded areas. They were joined by helicopters and men from RAF squadrons all over England. Drops were made by teams carrying survival gear, radios, stretchers, chainsaws, axes and ropes.

These men were often put down in places they couldn't find on a map for the storm had dramatically changed the character of the countryside. To many it looked like a Malaysian jungle or Burmese swamp rather than a quiet woodland hamlet in rural England.

Electricity Board divisional headquarters became the nerve centre of this massive operation. The demand for information caused its own problems for press officers had to feed radio, TV and newspapers, hungry for the news. Special emergency telephone enquiry centres were established to field the thousands of calls direct from customers. At Hythe in Kent, for example, there were more than 27,000 queries in less than a week.

Stories of tragedy, bravery and thoughtfulness were soon coming to light.

○ Electricity board staff in every region dropped their normal jobs to become accommodation officers.

○ Tonbridge School in Kent loaned blankets and sheets so that visiting engineers could sleep on the floor at a nearby training centre. Plastic lilos were bought from nearby shops.

○ All regions appealed on radio for offers of bed and breakfast. The great difficulty lay in the necessity to keep teams of linesmen under one roof if possible.

○ A family in Brasted Chart, Kent with solid fuel central heating put a notice on the gate offering hot baths and showers. Their story was told in London Weekend's Six O'clock Show.

○ Farmers rang in desperation seeking help for their animals. Right across southern England many had to milk cows by hand and with herds of 5,000 or more this became a daunting experience. A pig breeder in Sussex was unable to feed his 8,000 animals.

○ A hotel in Penshurst offered two elegant four-poster beds for engineers. The offer was turned down because Seeboard felt the hotel could not cope with such muddy wellies!

○ Sadly there were many tragedies. A visiting linesman from Merseyside died at East Horam, Sussex and another linesman from Licolnshire was killed at Haywards Heath.

○ Southern Electricity Board served nearly 2,500 meals for people without power and then took the unusual step of taking advertisements to thank people for their patience.

Nothing of any height stood in the face of the storm. Here in Upper Beeding, Sussex a pylon toppled taking with it many miles of overhead line. In other areas poles were smashed like matchwood, transformers and other distribution equipment came crashing to the ground.

Not far from this spot Duke William's Norman conquerors met King Harold's English warriors in the most famous conflict in history. This picture shows another conflict — the fight to clear the road and restore power against horrendous odds. This is Battle, East Sussex, a few days after Black Friday.

Teams of trained men arrived in helicopters carrying the necessary survival gear.

Linesmen in Essex show how teamwork can help in a crisis.

Wind Speeds

Station / Area	*Highest Reported 10 Minute Mean Speed during 00 to 13 GMT on 16 Oct 1987		*Approximate Return Period of Mean Speed in Years	Highest Reported Gust Speed during 00 to 13 GMT on 16 Oct 1987		Approximate Return Period of Gust Speed in Years
	Knots	MPH		Knots	MPH	
Brize Norton (Oxon)	25	29	Less than 10	50	58	Less than 10
Oxford	35	40	Not available	62	71	Not available
Boscombe Down (Salisbury)	36	41	Less than 10	70	81	20
Hurn (Bournemouth Airport)	37	43	10	62	71	10
Southampton Weather Centre	48	55	Not available	75	86	Not available
St Catherines (Isle of Wight)	58	67	Not available	90	104	Not available
Jersey (Channel Isles)	55	63	10	85	98	15
Herstmonceux (Eastbourne)	60	69	Not available	90	104	Not available
Langdon Bay (Dover)	62	71	Not available	90	104	Not available
Manston (Margate)	61	70	Over 500	86	99	Over 200
East Malling (Kent)	37	43	Not available	74	85	Not available
Gravesend (Kent)	34	39	Not available	74	85	Not available
Gatwick (West Sussex)	34	39	Less than 10	86	99	Over 300
London Airport	39	45	20	66	76	40
London Weather Centre	44	51	200	82	94	120
Stansted Airport	34	39	10	65	75	20
Shoeburyness (Essex)	55	63	Over 500	87	100	Over 500
Wattisham (Stowmarket)	48	55	45	72	83	10
Hemsby (Great Yarmouth)	45	52	Not available	78	90	Not available

* Strictly the Mean Speed over *1 hour* should be used to calculate the Return Period.
 However as such data are not yet available the '10 Minute' (synoptic) mean Speed has been taken as the best available guide.

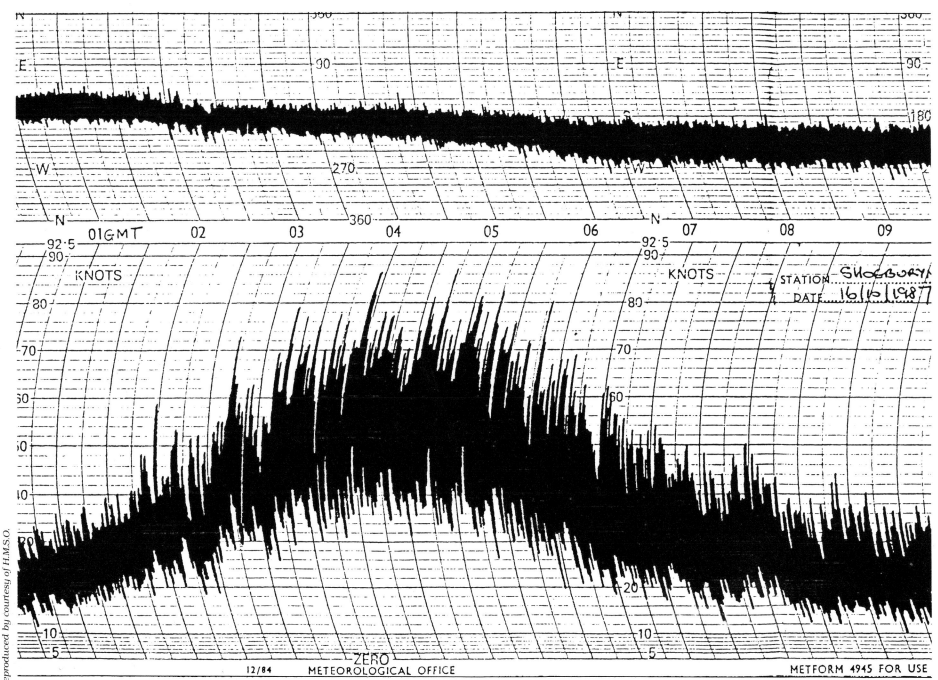

Copy of the Anemogram (wind record) for Shoeburyness (Essex), on October 16, 1987.

How the churches suffered

At the height of the storm church spires and steeples came crashing down all over south-east England causing damage running into millions of pounds. Many famous landmarks were lost and some of the country's oldest churches badly battered.

The 100 foot church spire of St Mary's, Minster (in Thanet) collapsed into the churchyard in a tangled heap of ancient timbers and masonry. St Mary's was built in 1027 shortly after the landing of St Augustine and is famous for its fine interior.

The spire of Rotherfield parish church, another landmark for miles around, and believed to be 360 years old, also collapsed. In numerous churchyards, gravestones were lifted out of the ground, headstones smashed and precious stained glass windows broken by flying debris. Churchyard yew trees were lucky if they survived.

New churches also suffered. St Justus at Rochester completely disintegrated at the height of the storm causing damage estimated at more than £300,000. The poignant picture on page 107 illustrates the total chaos.

Diocesan officials in several counties are still carefully assessing the extent of the damage and appealing for help from the local communities.

The Restoration

FIFTEEN million trees were blow down by the hurricane according to the action committee set up by the Forestry Commission to assess the extent of the disaster. Worst affected counties were Kent, Sussex and Surrey and for the 4,000 landowners in that corner of England life is still far from normal.

Woodland trusts, local authorities and landowners will all play their full part in restoring the ravaged countryside but the task is enormous and very long term. In most cases little progress can be made without financial assistance.

Throughout the winter, landowners have been busy repairing fences to prevent animals from straying, and opening up new walks. Not all the familiar, more popular paths are open yet but in time we will all be trudging along those well-used arteries for our pleasure and leisure.

This time though some woods will be impenetrable and the landscape will have changed perhaps beyond our recognition.

Photograph: Surrey Mirror

The stained-glass windows in ancient Burstow church were smashed. Outside, boughs crashed against the church tower.

Telegraph poles and trees lie side by side. In the background is St Paul's Church, Swanley, which was damaged by more falling pines.

Gravestones were lifted in this churchyard near Brighton.

The 65 ft tall shingled spire of Rotherfield Parish Church, a landmark for miles around, collapsed in a tangle of twisted timbers before the fury of the gale. Damage to the 360-year-old spire, was estimated at more than £25,000.

A large cedar in the grounds of a neighbouring manor came crashing down narrowly missing St Nicholas Church, Compton, which dates back to 987.

A wooden cross is carried from a wrecked building which was once a church. St Justus, Rochester looks more like the victim of a wartime bomb.

Photograph: Isle of Thanet Gazette

The 100 foot church spire of St Mary's Minster collapsed into the churchyard. St Mary's is one of the oldest churches in Thanet, built shortly after the landing of St Augustine. Nearby the 14th century St John's Church also suffered.

Photograph: David Bennett

Flooded farm land near Brighton, Sussex.

Part of a minaret, weighing two tons, blasted through the roof of the Royal Pavilion at Brighton interrupting a £9 million restoration programme. No-one was hurt but the damage was extensive.

The Mayfair Hotel, Jersey which lost its entire roof in the storm.

A car in Essex which took the fall of a mighty sycamore tree.

Light aircraft at Biggin Hill airport were upended by the hurricane like toy planes and the bill for the damage is expected to run into thousands of pounds. Among the losers was the Biggin Hill School of Flying. Three light aircraft, worth £20,000 each, were completely written off. One plane was lifted off the ground and landed on top of another. It was a similar story at the Air Training Club where four light aircraft were completely destroyed.

Photographs: Evening Argus and Thanet Gazette

Biggin Hill was not the only airport to suffer heavy losses. Light aircraft at Brighton (top) and Margate were turned upside down by the force of the wind.

Sappers in their British army combat smocks are almost camouflaged against the fallen foliage as they help to restore power lines.

Army to the Rescue

SOLDIERS from the legendary Gurkha Rifle Regiment, whose Nepalese ancestors swore allegiance to Britain many years ago, brought their famous fighting qualities to the most rural areas of Kent and Sussex and immediately felt at home in the dense but decimated woodland.

The Gurkhas were backing South Eastern Electricity Board's battle against hurricane damage. Armed with their famous fighting knives, the Kukri, they hacked their way through the undergrowth, worked in unison with local authority contractors and cleared the way for linesmen and later Telecom engineers.

In the densely wooded area of West Chiltington and Storrington where the Gurkhas were split into three groups, they missed their special four-day religious festival, Dwali and in the Westerham area of West Kent they joined their military colleagues from the Royal Engineers at Chatham in clearing fallen trees from an area 800 feet above sea level.

Other soldiers, not so well trained in jungle warfare, brought their tools, skills and cheerful enthusiasm to the aid of southern England. In Hampshire and West Sussex soldiers, camping rough, and working in terrible weather conditions toiled alongside neighbours clearing the A3 where an estimated 500 trees blocked a 20-mile stretch between Petersfield and Milford.

Further north in East Anglia soldiers from the Royal Border Regiment and the Royal Engineers helped to clear the way for the Eastern Electricity Board. In Norfolk, the army drove in on the Sunday morning complete with a giant recovery vehicle capable of lifting 12 tonnes and winching up to 23 tonnes.

Within a few weeks overhead power lines were in place and the army turned their attention to the task facing Telecom. The job of restoring cables and poles split and ripped in the storm took a little longer and many people throughout the south-east were without a telephone for more than a month.

Water supplies too were hard hit and again it was the villages and hamlets which suffered the brunt of the disaster. Pumping ceased as a result of interruptions to electricity supplies, and tree-damaged or burst water mains meant that families and old people were left without lighting, heating, water or basic communications for days.

Photograph: David Bennett

Gurkhas used their Kukris (fighting knives), to help with tree clearance.

123

This could be the Burmese swamp, the Amazon jungle or the African bush. Little wonder our soldiers were confused.

Many roads were clear within days but on the hillside the soldiers fought on with fallen pines.

Corporal Mick Yeomans and Lance Corporal Tim Kusick begin to remove fallen trees near Ide Hill. Their task was daunting.

Beech Lodge, Ide Hill was totally marooned by fallen trees and it took almost two weeks for the Griffiths family to be liberated by soldiers from the Royal Engineers.

The glory of Seal Chart in Kent as it looked earlier this century. In later years the trees grew together to form a long avenue.

128

The same area of Seal Chart as it looks today.

Polesden Lacey, near Dorking, formerly the home of Richard Sheridan, the dramatist, suffered badly in the storm. The 30 acres of woodland were decimated and it will take many more months to restore the Walk designed by Sheridan.

Photograph: Alex Watson, Sevenoaks Chronicle

Knole Park, Sevenoaks after the clearance. A forest of trees, many of them ancient oaks and beeches, has vanished.

Before and after. Trees on the Pantiles at Tunbridge Wells which stood the test of time, failed the trial of the storm.

Grief Forgotten

AS the grass grows, the song birds sing and the scarred earth yields its fruits again, the violent ordeal of October 16, 1987 will gradually fade from the mind. For wildlife, too, it will be like a grief forgotten.

How many animals perished in the storm we shall never know. Dead starlings were found in streets along the south coast and black-headed gulls were discovered impaled on wire fences. Birds flying south to winter in England may have flown directly into the face of the gale and the loss of nesting holes was considerable.

Conservationists, however, believe that most birds managed to ride out the winds. They also believe that the timing was important; just like people sleeping, most birds were generally roosting although some were blown from their preferred haunts to other areas. An albatross suddenly appeared on the Norfolk coast and Sabine's gulls, usually a rarity in Britain, were seen in East Anglia.

The storm provided a few light-hearted situations. Rambo, an oversexed Jacob ram was delighted when the gale destroyed the fence protecting a herd of pedigree sheep. At the height of the storm he wandered into the woolly compound next door for a night of wild passion. The owner of the ewes says he will claim damages in the spring when the lambs are born.

The windows of the London Butterfly House in Syon Park, Brentford were smashed allowing many beautiful specimens to escape. Two rare South African butterflies, with a wing span of seven inches, survived by eating rotten fruit from a nearby garden and falling into a drunken stupor. They were found and returned to the Butterfly House.

At Howletts Zoo Park, Canterbury, Xiang, a seven-year-old Clouded Leopard escaped and roamed free in the area for seven days. Eventually, hungry and bedraggled he was baited with dead chicken and reunited with his keeper. The delightful picture on page 11 is the first moment of togetherness.

The effect of the storm lingered on for several days. With trees still blocking village roads and fences destroyed, a couple at Fawke Common, near Sevenoaks found themselves in the middle of a living nightmare when their horse, investigating areas normally out of bounds, trod on the cover of the swimming pool and crashed into the deep end with a spectacular splash.

His owners spent several hours in the pool, first coaxing him to the shallow end and then trying to pull him out. Unable to call for help (the roads were blocked and the phone was out of action) they eventually built a staircase of straw bales and breeze blocks and the terrified horse, at the point of collapse, was able to escape from his long ordeal.

Photograph: The National Trust

The 200 acres of woodland belonging to the National Trust at Toys Hill suffered 90 per cent losses as the wind seared across the greensand ridge felling trees like matchwood. Picture shows Toys Hill warden, Geordie Prest describing his plight to Prince Charles who is carrying a copy of the first edition of this book.

133

Woodlands throughout Southern England have taken a heavy toll. Some trees have been snapped off like matchsticks, others uprooted or reduced to skeletons. Mick Martin, Head Gardener at Scotney contemplates the scene with Bruno at his side.

Photograph: Holly Pelling

A familiar sight throughout Southern England. Logs are piled up by the roadside before being taken away for pulp. Nature is making a come-back, as the foreground shows.

While trees all around were crashing during the storm this 1,000 year-old oak at Stonewall Park, Chiddingstone Hoath survived. Mr and Mrs Frank May pictured here soon after the hurricane remember an expert from Kew Gardens examining the tree several years ago and assessing its age.

Anthony and Barbara Penman with the remains of the 400-year-old oak which fell on their house.

136

Photograph: Courier Newspapers

Insurance companies who boast that they "never make a drama out of a crisis" were almost eating their words as massive claims poured into their offices in the days following the storm. These pictures show two homes badly damaged and the necessity for immediate repair. It will be some time yet before official figures show the full extent of the losses and the effect on future premiums.

137

Duncan and Lisa from Halstead, Kent fill their pockets with acorns. These have now been resown in their school grounds in the hope that they will flourish into mighty oaks.

Clare Friend, aged six, who is a pupil at Ightham primary school helped to plant an oak sapling at Crown Point, Seal to mark Kent County Council's Replant the Garden of England appeal.

Ask what you please; look where you will,
you cannot get to the bottom of the resources of Britain.
No demand is too novel or too sudden to be met.
No need is too unexpected to be supplied.
No strain is too prolonged for the patience of our people.
No suffering or peril daunts their hearts.

Winston S. Churchill 1918

About the Author . . .

BOB Ogley has been a newspaperman for 32 years, editor of the Sevenoaks Chronicle for 18, suffered all the vicissitudes of local journalism climbed to some of its heights and enjoyed a long, unfinished crusade on behalf of his newspaper and town.

For him, 1987 was a memorable year. In January, along with the rest of Sevenoaks and district, he was marooned by blizzards. In April he cycled from John O'Groats to Lands End and raised more than £4,000 for local charities. During the summer he enjoyed the privilege of raising four foxcubs before returning them to the wild. In October he was isolated again, this time by hundreds of fallen trees around his home near Toys Hill, Kent.

Bob's decision to hire an aircraft from Biggin Hill was rewarded with some of the finest aerial photographs of a natural disaster and the shot of the fallen oaks which give Sevenoaks its name was a piece of instant history.

Inspired by the success of his "hurricane edition", Bob set out to record the events and the aftermath of Friday October 16 in a book of photographs with a sprinkling of text. In the Wake of The Hurricane was an immediate hit and in the three weeks leading up to Christmas sold almost 20,000 copies.

The interest in Bob's book continued in the New Year. It was a best seller in bookshops all over the south-east and orders were received in other parts of England. In the Sunday Times of January 24 it was listed as the nation's sixth most popular non-fiction paperback, a phenomenal achievement for a "local book".

The original seven oaks at Sevenoaks which were felled in 1956.

140